I0481506

Outsourcing Blueprint Guide

Ralph Campbell

Copyright © Book Skim Publishing

All rights reserved. No part of this publication may be reproduced, distributed, or transmitted in any form or by any means, including photocopying, recording, or other electronic or mechanical methods, without the prior written permission of the publisher, except in the case of brief quotations embodied in critical reviews and certain other non-commercial uses permitted by copyright law.

Bookskim Publishing

623 Collins Street

Melbourne, Victoria, 3000

Australia

www.bookskim.com

contact@bookskim.com

Get This As a FREE Audiobook via Amazon's Audible.com

Visit:
Bookskim.com/free

Introduction

If you are new to Internet marketing, you are probably doing everything yourself. By now you've probably come to the conclusion that there's not enough time in a day to do it all.

More importantly you're probably realizing that you could make more money by freeing up time so you can work in areas where your *real* talents lie, such as establishing joint ventures, driving traffic or placing ads.

Outsourcing is the logical solution to freeing up your jammed schedule and long to-do list. Most new marketers start out multi-tasking to the point where nothing ever gets done properly, or worse, your work gets backed up and never finished.

Part of this frenetic focus is a desire to learn all the new techniques and processes as fast as you can and then to apply it to start the stream of income you want.

The blunt fact is that if you try to do everything yourself your business will at best stop growing, and at worse, go under.

You need to outsource some of the tasks that other people could do for you, equally as well if not better. For example can you *really* answer an email asking for a lost download link so much better than anyone else?

This guide will show you what you need to know about outsourcing the tasks that you need for the success of your business but don't have the time or expertise to do everything your business demands. When you start needing help you have three choices.

➢ You can hire a permanent staff member that works with you on a daily or weekly basis.

➢ You can hire an online virtual assistant to handle your overload. They will do your bookkeeping, ghostwriting and most any other chore you don't want to do.

➢ Or you can outsource your extra work piece-by-piece, on an as-needed basis.

Let's take a look at those options.

Should You Hire Permanent Help?

Internet marketers often need help, but the vast majority of them are not in a financial position to afford one, particularly when they first start out with an online business. As simple as most make starting an online business seem, the truth is that the more successful you become, the more work there is to get done.

Multiple sites, blogs or memberships require steady attention and updating. As an internet marketer you have to stay in contact with your growing list of subscribers or customers, which requires email and a series of auto responder messages.

Do you really have time to write those emails and auto responder messages?

And if you do, couldn't you pay someone to do it for you, just as well, while freeing you up to do the things that actually generate the income for your business?

If you hire a *real* permanent assistant (someone who works for you as an employee), your next task is setting up the payroll and necessary payroll taxes and possibly insurance, checking local employment regulations and arranging for holidays and vacation leave.

You more than likely will have to share your home office or work space with your employee. You will also have to spend a portion of your evening setting up the tasks you want your assistant to handle the next day.

If you've ever hired staff you'll know that it can be a legal and financial nightmare. It's so much easier to use *remote* workers who are self-employed and work for you as and when you need them.

One solution that is becoming popular with online marketers is to hire virtual assistant. They are talented multi-faceted professionals who can handle your administrative and clerical duties, along with providing support for you as you need it. Some offer marketing services like article writing, answering emails, and researching.

Some Virtual Assistants have specialties you never thought about, like fluency in foreign languages. They can be your bookkeeper, secretary, "gofer," researcher, desktop publisher or project manager. Since they work over the Internet, physical location is not a problem. Contact will be via email, fax, phone and, if necessary, snail mail.

A very good option for several reasons is hiring a freelancer when you need a specific task completed and outsourcing will speed up the process. The major benefit of hiring a freelancer is being able to utilize their talents as you need them. Your only expense is their fee for finishing your job, which was negotiated before they accepted your job.

Most freelancers specialize in one specific area, like writing e-books, developing e-courses, producing sales letters or programming software. Others will design and put your website online and make it work for you. You can hire a freelancer to create your customer support desk and run it for you. *If your need can imagine it, you can probably find a freelancer to do it.*

When you hire a freelancer, you will find that their practices vary widely. Some will require you to sign a written contract or request deposits. They may charge you by the page, day or per project. While a flat rate or a fee is most common, some are using a value-based pricing method, which is calculated on the apparent value of the project to the client.

When a freelancer completes a project for you, they usually do not have any rights to the copyright for their work, including any e-book or e-course they wrote to your specifications.

It falls under the category of "works for hire" which is defined by US copyright law, specifically Section 101, Copyright Act of 1976 (USC 17 §101) –(Chapter 2, §201). Other countries might have different regulations.

Freelancers are commonly very well-versed in the latest Internet trends that change frequently. They have to stay current in order to provide the best service to you when you need outsourcing. Effectively, when you use a freelancer to outsource your jobs, you are often (although not always) getting a very high quality of work for much less money than hiring an employee.

Depending on your budget, you can outsource your projects one at a time or several at once to different freelancers. Most freelancers are highly motivated, because it's in their interest to provide a high standard of work -if you are more than satisfied with their work, you might use them again. Since they work on an "as-needed" basis, they do not have a stable income like a salaried employee might have.

The good news for you as a 'virtual employer' is that there are far more freelancers than work available.

There is a possible downside to hiring freelancers when you need outsourcing.

Some people take payment then disappear. I try to solve this problem by paying 50% up front then 50% on completion but it still happens, although the vast majority of outsource workers are extremely reliable.

Communication delays can be another downside if you don't plan for it. For the most part, you will be dealing with your freelancer by email, which is close to instant you will have to consider time zones and geographical location. Your work day might be your freelancer's sleep time if they are in another country than you are, which would get your email opened the next day.

The possible email delay also means that questions and answers would also be at the mercy of location and time zones. As clear as your explanation and requirements for your finished product were initially, there will usually be points that need further clarification as your project moves through the creation process.

A viable solution to this time delay could be Skype, which is a worldwide free phone service over the Internet. You could set up times when you both would be available if questions needed answers or your freelancer had a confusion that needed attention.

Though your freelancer might make it seem like you are the only client he has at the moment, he's probably working for several clients at one time or one client with several jobs. While your project might be your only focus, freelancers are running a business just like you and you might have to share his time with others.

Some might agree to an exclusive arrangement, but it will more than likely cost more money than it would if you were sharing his focus with other marketers just like you.

To avoid misunderstandings, get a clear and precise contract that states your expected completion date, what content you want included, who does the research, direct contact methods for both of you, fees and payment dates, to name a few important details.

It would be a good idea to give some thought to possible illnesses or computer disasters that could happen to anyone at anytime and delay the completion of your project. Think about starting your freelancer on your project with enough lead time to cover unavoidable delays. Freelancers are people and stuff happens to people that cannot be controlled.

Most highly successful marketers use outsourcing to support their multiple businesses. Copy Success!

Want to see how to create a $1,000,000 with outsourcing?

Read on.

Can Outsourcing Make You $1,000,000?

Yes, it can, but probably not overnight.

Most new Internet marketers start out on a very limited budget.

It feels 'dangerous' to outsource when your budget is so limited, more so if you're someone who likes to keep 'control' of your business.

All I can say to this is that every single marketer I've spoken to about outsourcing say they'll never go back to doing everything in their business again. I have to agree, although the first time you outsource something it's a scary thing.

Some things are more important to outsource on a budget that others.

For example I would always outsource good quality website and e-book graphics (these sell products) with my last $50 rather than try to do a (bad) job myself.

It's false economy because it would harm my product in the long run.

There are lots of details to cover and techniques you need to learn when you want to put up a website (sales letter) to sell your product. All of them can be covered with outsourcing. But, for your first product, let's continue with ideas about getting it online for little money or none —starting your first step toward your million-dollar paycheck.

Blogs can be your first and possibly your most lucrative method to sell your products. They can be put online for free and are very popular with the browsing public. Don't just throw up a blog and expect to make money. Give it some thought.

Pick your subject carefully, making sure it is one you will enjoy working with and that you have some knowledge and expertise with it. Create your first product and a free report on the same subject to give away to those who subscribe to your blog. If you know nothing about blogs and the widgets they use for optimal design, this might be a good time to outsource.

If your first business project gets online with all aspects working the way they are supposed to work, your life will be easier.

Once you have a profitable system in place, outsourcing will become more important for your success. Outsourcing actually means that you will have more time to handle the business side of your blog and to keep the money flowing in.

That's the reason you started an online business in the first place, isn't it? Tending to the tedious daily chores will just reduce the amount of time you need to make more money or to keep the income flow moving.

Let's look at that process in more detail.

Work your first site or blog until you find a method that starts making money for you. Keep at it for several weeks to make sure it is going to continue to make money. Once you are pretty sure that you have a workable process, outsource the tedious jobs that take your time away from making money and tie it up for maintenance and customer service.

Let's look at some numbers that will illustrate why you need to outsource when you are making money.

Suppose you have a set of five videos that show your subscribers how to market a product. You can send them one free video each week with specific steps for separate procedures in the marketing process. After they get the last video, you can market your related or other products to them by email.

Let's say your squeeze page converts browsers into buyers at 35% and you can send 100 visitors to your squeeze page every day. That's 245 new subscribers every week and 980 every month. If you send an offer for one of your products to each one of those new subscribers, you could expect varied results, but the numbers would make you money.

For example, if your email got opened by 40% of those 980 new subscribers, you would have 392 subscribers looking at your product. If 50% opened your email, that number increases to 490 and to 588 at 60%.

Not everyone who reads your email and follows your link to the product is going to buy it. An average conversion rate is 3% of those who view your product offer. Using the subscriber numbers in the previous paragraph, if 3% of your 392 subscribers buy your product, that's 12 new sales every month. For 490 subscribers, you would have 15 new monthly sales and 18 for 588 subscribers.

If your product sold for $20, that's a monthly income of $240, $300 or $360. If your price is higher or lower, do the maths yourself to see what your projected monthly income would be.

How would outsourcing help you increase your monthly income?

If you outsourced your tedious daily tasks, you could spend your time improving your marketing techniques and creating new products to put in your arsenal of products to sell. If you could outsource traffic generation to an expert, a freelancer well-versed in traffic generation methods, you could earn an extra $100 a month while you were doing other, more lucrative tasks.

Using the same numbers above, an extra $100 a month would net you $340, $400 or $460. The yearly income would be $4080 to $5520. Just remember that those figures are the example result of outsourcing your tedious traffic-generation chores for one blog.

Doesn't sound like much income to you? Multiply it by the monthly number of new sites or blogs you plan on setting up in the next few months.

Commonly, you would have to work your tail off for several months to get that $100 a month increase in your income. If you are constant in using good techniques to generate traffic and offering good products to your subscribers, you could be in a position very quickly to hire a reputable ghostwriter to produce articles for you that will start your viral marketing campaign.

Your ghostwriter could relieve you of the entire process, researching, writing, submitting to article directories. All those processes are very time-consuming.

For easy computation, let's say you hired a ghostwriter to write and submit 10 articles for you every week. If each article brought 20 visitors to your blog who subscribed, that would be 200 more subscribers each week, or 800 a month. To continue, if your products sold for $20 and your conversion rate was a very conservative 3%, you would make $480 additional return each month.

Your numbers and income would increase if you also hired a freelancer experienced in traffic generation. Initially, the ghostwriting fees and what you would have to pay a freelancer for generating more traffic to your site might eat deeply into your profits, but each new subscriber actually equals more opportunities for marketing multiple products.

In a nutshell, you pay a ghostwriter $10 to write and submit a quality article for you and that generates 10 visitors who subscribe and eventually buy your $20 product. Your $200 increase in sales would more than cover the $10 cost of one article. Simple math for increasing incomes.

Your outsourcing fees would remain the same, if you don't increase the number of freelancers on your payroll, while your product sales will keep growing. That wouldn't happen very easily if you had to do all the chores yourself.

One successful business model is to invest your profits back into your business and increasing your outsourcing in other areas that consume your time. You already know that spending money on outsourcing will increase your profit margin.

It is possible to outsource all parts of your business, including everyday maintenance. The potential for creating a 7-figure income is quite possible with the help of freelancers and outsourcers.

Many marketers (myself included) act as middlemen, providing a service but using outsourcers to provide the work.

Put (very) simply –if I offer a traffic generation service where I promise 300 new subscribers every month through my service, I might charge a $500 monthly fee. If I can outsource this subscriber generation work to an SEO expert (for example) I might have to pay him $350 a month.

That gives me $150 profit.

Not great but suppose I have 30 clients for my service.

That means after paying my outsource worker I have $4500 profit.

Not too bad for very (very) little work.

Outsourcing every task that was profitable for you originally, will continue to be profitable. If Internet trends or techniques change, just change with them. Your outsourcers will know how to do that. They might be invisible and working quietly for you in the background, but they are professionals.

At some point, you could even hire (outsource) a project manager to take care of all your outsourcing needs and manage your business for you. Your goal of a $1,000,000 business can be reached almost hands-free if you outsource with professionals.

Now that you know the value of outsourcing let's look at some common mistakes many marketers make when they first hire a freelancer.

How To Avoid These 7 Outsourcing Mistakes

Truthfully, most marketers make mistakes when they start to outsource. I did –but I saw it –and still do –as a learning process.

Here are 7 major outsourcing mistakes and how to avoid them:

Mistake #1: Expecting outsourcers to work the same way you do and at the same speed and level. In short – expecting them to 'be' you...

Your work habits will not be the same as someone else's. A lot of marketers make this simple mistake and that can cause misunderstandings when you hire a freelancer to help you.

Don't expect freelancers to work as fast as you work and to know what you know. They won't. Neither would you if the shoe was on the other foot. Don't expect too much.

The solution is to make it as clear as possible what you want doing, and to show them any examples of the kind of work that you've done yourself in the past.

Don't clarify your needs verbally. That leads to oversights and costly mistakes. Write it down. This also means you can keep a copy to refer back to if there are any problems in the future.

For example: if you want specific keywords used with a precise percentage on each page, say so. If you want a certain type of keyword used, like long-tail keywords to target a specific target, be explicit in your explanation of your needs. Tell them and then ask them to explain it back to you in their own words to ensure they really do understand.

The more you share with your freelancer, the better the product you order will be when you get it. Mind reading is not normally an outsourcer's talent.

Mistake #2: Not outsourcing the correct things.

If your blog is widely read because of your 'quirky' or 'personal' style don't try to outsource this. In short don't try to outsource any part of your business that is 'you'. In my opinion this would include things like video presentations, webinars, mentoring and anything where the customer pays for 'you.

So, if you are a poor writer but a good speaker, outsource the e-book.

The ideal solution would be to dictate the e-book and then get a freelancer to transcribe it for you.

Mistake #3: Setting lax deadlines or none at all

Meeting deadlines is difficult at times for anyone, particularly those working full-time from home. When you tire of a project, your motivation to complete a project might be weakening. Your focus could be distracted by the pretty day or the desire to just sit on the couch and watch some TV. After all, you're the boss and no one is telling you what to do and when to do it.

Remember when you are hiring a freelancer that they are working from home, too, and have the same distractions and lack of motivation at times that you have. Since you are paying your freelancer, you can set clear and strict deadlines for delivery of your completed project.

If your project is large, for example 50 articles or a long e-book, set checkpoints for delivery of finished sections of your project. That will allow you to check the quality of the work

while it is ongoing and give you time to make adjustments if you and your freelancer didn't understand each other at the beginning.
Tell them what you want, when you want it and what it should entail.

Then get them to explain it back to you.

Clarity is the one biggest factor that can make or break your outsourcing endevours.

Mistake #4: Not being thorough about checking the completed work

This step in the freelance process is very common with busy marketers.

The real result of not checking the completed work very carefully is the hit your reputation will take if it's got grammar errors or misspellings. The quality might not be what you expected to get from a freelancer with good recommendations.

For all you know, the freelancer outsourced the work to another ghostwriter with less skills than the one you hired demonstrated. This really shocked me the first time I came across this!

The content might not be unique and, for all you know, it might be plagiarized from another writer's product. Check for validity by using Internet services to check out the uniqueness of the content, like Copyscape. (http://www.copyscape.com/)

You're not being suspicious –you're protecting your business.

Another valuable, free technique is to take a couple of sentences from your e-book or article and search for it on Google. If Google returns hits, you possibly have a plagiarized product.

Some freelancing communities or groups use an escrow account to protect both the freelancer and the marketer from unethical behavior. Most freelancers will accept 50% upfront and the rest upon delivery.

The buzzwords for this mistake are: Check! Check! Check!

Mistake #5: Not treating a good freelancer like gold

You will not find good freelancers on every corner of the Web. When you do find one that meet your requirements, fits your style and understands your needs, keep them happy with you. Freelancers with those qualities will be difficult to find.

Some clients act like they are the boss in a normal business when they hire a freelancer. Most freelancers work full-time for themselves for the same reason you do.

The message here is to treat your freelancer like a treasured part of your business and not like an hourly employee. Normal praise is nice to hear for good work. If you need some part of your project adjusted, don't blanket criticize the freelancer, but point out the areas that need some improvement and give them time to do it. If you provide an occasional small cash reward or quality work, you will have a loyal freelancer who will make sure your interests are taken care of.

Don't accept shoddy work from any freelancer you hire though. It's your business and reputation that will suffer.

Mistake #6: Believing that quality is guaranteed by a high price

It is a common human belief that the good stuff costs more. That might apply to automobiles and wine, but not necessarily to ghostwriting and computer programming.

International outsourcing companies are proving to be very good at ghostwriting. In places like, India or another country with a low cost of living, outsourcing prices are likely to be very affordable. American and UK writers might charge many time more than writers in emerging countries, but their work is not necessarily better.

Think about it. The cost of living determines the price of almost any service anywhere. Location does not determine quality.

Mistake #7: Putting All Your Eggs In One Basket

When marketers discover a truly good freelancer who delivers a quality product rapidly, always meets or betters their deadlines, is affordable and easy to work with, the common result is to give that freelancer more work. Eventually, you will be tempted to give them all your work.

This is fine for your production and bottom line, but it puts you in a bind if your freelancer gets ill, goes on a vacation or has family emergencies that require all his attention and attendance. That pretty upward line on your income forecasts will flat line in a minute.

Smart marketers hire several quality freelancers and spread their work out between them. That's not being disloyal to your original freelancer, but being a smart marketer with a good business sense.

There are many more lazy business practices that could be added here, but the major 7 mistakes are the major problems that will make the most difference, positive or negative, to your business.

Let's determine what you can outsource in the next chapter.

What Can You Outsource?

It's tempting to outsource everything. Why not? It makes you feel like Donald Trump as you imagine a stress-free business and huge income!

Consider this first....

To start with you should outsource online three basic categories...

> ➤ The **tedious tasks** that you have to do over and over on a daily basis, like daily posting on your blog, answering questions from your customers or submitting articles to directories. All of these tasks take a lot of your time, and can *often* be done just as well by a freelancer.

➢ **Any chore you don't want to do** is a great candidate for outsourcing. When you are buried in multiple details that needs addressing or fixing by you and you don't like doing any of it, you have a great list for outsourcing. Not enjoying your work will turn it into drudgery and stop your progress. This isn't laziness – it's *knowing your business and your strengths*.

➢ When you have **work you cannot do**or don't know how to do, what choice do you have? Outsourcing is your only option, even if you pay the kid next door to design a header or hire a graphic artist in Romania. When you pay someone to do the work you need done, it is outsourcing. If you can't do it yourself and it needs doing –outsource it.

Most successful Internet marketers will tell you that, in order to be successful your have to work "AT" your business and not "IN" it. As a business owner, your job is to keep your business on track. That means you will have to stay current with emerging and vanishing trends. When new techniques surface on the Internet, you will have to know about them and how to use them in your business.

Successful business owners spend most of their time doing those tasks.

Tedious details will distract you from making sure your business is running on the cutting edge and providing products your customers want.

One of the most tedious and repetitious jobs marketers have to do is keyword research. You can easily spend hours online researching keywords pertinent to your niche and checking a seemingly endless list of related keywords.

Hire an expert with keyword research and free up your time. You will get the results you need a lot quicker than doing it yourself. Your expert or freelancer will give you a list of keywords pertinent to your business. All you have to do is pick out the ones you want to use and give them to your freelance writers.

Another thing you have to do is recognize that you might have the "employee mindset," which keeps you thinking that you have to be able to do everything.

For example, social bookmarking is a hot marketing tool that can explode your business by driving targeted traffic to your sites. It takes hours to bookmark every piece of your content on all the popular social bookmarking sites. This is a prime reason for outsourcing.

This is a pretty complete list of normal **tedious (for many people) tasks** that you should consider outsourcing as soon as you can:

➢ **Writing Articles** that will start your viral marketing campaign and create your reputation as an expert in your niche.

➢ **Submitting Articles to Directories** takes up a lot of time. No directory has the same requirements and restrictions. Few have similar formatting pages to use for posting articles for approval.

➢ **Social Bookmarking** is so hot as a traffic generation source that it should be in flames. Everybody is flocking to any of over 300 sites to build their lists, create a reputation and sell products. The only problem that just screams outsourcing is bookmarking every piece of content you have. That could take hours and hours every single day.

➢ **Creating Accounts** at every article directory and social bookmarking site will keep you busy for the better part of

- ➢ entire days. Few are the same as any others and all can be cantankerous at time, which might require more than one attempt to accomplish actual registration. Freelancers will love to do this for you.

- ➢ **Submitting Video and Audio** to websites is no easier than submitting anything else to a directory or social bookmarking site. You have to find sites or directories that want your products and wade through their submission policies. Outsource it.

Of course there are other tasks that would be better outsourced by you. They will pop up from time to time. Keep your list of trusted freelancers close to you.

When you start collecting tasks you hate doing it will be time to think of outsourcing them to someone who likes doing it. A few necessary tasks that are easy to hate are article submissions, opening accounts at directories and social bookmarking sites. The reasons have been well discussed above. There are lots of others that you might hate just as passionately as those few mentioned.

Instead of fighting to finish tasks you detest and, as a result, probably will do a sloppy or incomplete job of it just to get it over with, outsource. You will be a lot happier and get more done on any day. You would do a better job if you could spend your time attracting joint venture partners or testing marketing ideas, for example.

This list is **tasks you might hate** and could easily outsource. Some tasks in each one of the three basic categories might overlap because different people hate different things.

- ➢ **Article Writing** is difficult for a lot of people. It isn't a character flaw but a different mind set or abilities.

- ➢ **Submitting Articles** would numb the mind of any person with an active and creative mind and consume entire days that could be better spent.

- ➢ **Product Creation** is pure joy to some and pure hell to others. It is tedious, requires hours of research at times, effective website design for sales and graphic capabilities for ebook covers, site headers, to name several tasks that might be hateful to you.

- ➢ **Account Creation** has been discussed in a couple of places in this chapter and

- it still stands as an exercise that will drive you crazy.

- **Creating Videos** might be the hot number on the Internet now, but they require several talents besides a camcorder. When you know that you need to create some to make your business more attractive, you will have to plan your content, have a script memorized, get appropriate screenshots ready for illustration when necessary, construct a "studio" for the actual recording and learn to use new software. There are very talented freelancers who can do the entire video for you and love every minute doing it. They would be well worth the money.

- **Turning Your Articles Into Podcasts** requires expertise you might not have or want to have. Giving the content to a freelancer will save your sanity and provide a professional product that will make you proud.

- **Copywriting** has been touted as the most valuable ability you can have if you are planning on marketing products online. Your sales copy is all that makes your site visitors buy your products. It is not the same as ghostwriting and

➢ requires a knowledge of verbal persuaders, how to make the benefits irresistible and how to create graphic touches that keep your visitors reading and moving down to the Buy Now button.

➢ **Website Design** is not an exercise in frivolous dancing clipart or flashing colors and raucous music. Your website is the presentation piece for your entire business. It has to be carefully designed and fulfill its purpose generating sales. This is not the job for a newbie.

➢ **Sales Letter & Squeeze Page Design** is another task better left to those who know how to do it. The mechanics are not that difficult but designing your squeeze page to fulfill its one and only purpose might be. The squeeze page is where you collect email addresses to build your marketing list. That's all it is supposed to do. If your sales copy is not effective or your bonus gift for signing up is not popular, you won't have a list, which means you also won't have a business.

➢ **Graphics Design** is an art form that doesn't belong to everyone with a website. You need professional headers,

> footers, ebook and ecourse covers, Buy Now buttons, even original bullets and arrows to rivet your reader's attention on your message.

Other services that could be hateful ones to you are customer service, forum management, link building with Search Engine Optimization (SEO) and blog creation, posting and commenting. Freelancers all over the world are waiting to help you with any of these tasks.

Work you can't do normally involves skills you don't have. Having a basic understanding of how to program software or how to design a kick ass website that sells products faster than you can create them is no easy feat. It requires experience and a thorough understanding of the physical and emotional processes required to move visitors into buyers.

Websites with the power to convert higher percentages of viewers into buyers need professional design. Copywriting is another critical skill that is better left to professionals until you know what you are doing.

This list has five processes that most cannot easily do without lots of experience and training and should be outsourced to professionals.

- ➤ **Copywriting** is a difficult skill that few master, Quite a few newcomers to Internet marketing slap together a website without a clue about what makes a compelling sales letter.

- ➤ **Website Design**, along with copywriting, is critical to your business and sales. Unless you know all the tricks and techniques that increase your conversion rate, outsourcing to a professional would make a difference in your sales.

- ➤ **Graphic Design** just has to be professional in all aspects or you will lose site visitors and business. There are so many great-looking websites on the Web that poorly designed graphics drive customers away from your website.

- ➤ **Programming** is a learned skill and it is not easy to use. If you want to create software for sale, you will have to learn to program complicated techniques flawlessly. Perfection in your software is absolutely required. Freelancing programmers are not difficult to find. Use them and your business will avoid lots of angry customers and requests for refunds.

- Even if you use a freelancer, test every program several times before putting it online. Enlist people on your list or people you trust to beta test your software. Test! Test! Test!

- Producing high quality videos is an art form that is not a natural ability most people have. Whatever you do, you do not want to have a clumsy, poorly produced video promoting your business. Once you lose customers it is difficult to get them back. Once you lose your credibility and professionalism, you might never get it back. Outsource!

The next chapter will discuss where to contact freelancers for outsourcing.

Where To Find Reliable Outsourcing

At one time there were only two or three places to find freelancers for your outsourcing needs. Now that outsourcing has become a 'respectable' Internet service, outsourcing websites can be found all over the world.

For more than several years, Elance.com was the most popular website to offer outsourcing to Internet marketers. It's still popular with those looking for freelancers, but, over the last few years, it has gained a lot of competition.

There are 6 popular outsourcing sites that dominate the freelancing business, but others are just as competent. One outsourcing site does not provide higher quality than another. Mostly, it boils down to personal preference.

Outsourcing websites bring together the freelancers and the employers. You would be an employer in this case. The website acts like a middle man for the selection process. Freelancers sign up, submit their credentials and check the lists for posted jobs that interest them. They will make bids on jobs they want to do.

As an employer, you will register with the site and post your jobs in correct categories. Your description of the job should be organized and complete. It will become the framework for the completion of your project. Freelancers will bid to get your job.

Many freelancers will enter low bids hoping to get selected. Good advice is to ignore the money bids and concentrate on the qualities listed in their profiles. They will state what they are good at and have testimonials from happy clients.

Read what other employers have said about the quality of their work. If they've posted a portfolio, check it out to make a judgment about their work.

Here's a list of the main outsourcing websites:

General Outsourcing:

Elance.com
Odesk.com
Guru.com
GetAFreelancer.com

Programming Outsourcing:

**ScriptLance.com
RentACoder.com**

A not so well-known resource is Amazon's service for Internet marketers, Mechanical Turk. This site is a marketplace to get tasks (jobs) performed that require human intelligence.

With the Mechanical Turk, you could post specifications for a job that required a series of 100 word paragraphs about a specific product. List the price you are willing to pay. Freelancers will find you.

Here's the link:
https://www.mturk.com/mturk/welcome

If you need fulltime help, you can hire freelancers on a fulltime basis by booking all or most of their time. If this is your plan and you are using freelancers from other countries, check the legalities before you make any offers.

The Philippines has become a player in the outsourcing business. Their reputation for providing quality work at a low price is building their credibility quickly. If you want to hire a freelancer fulltime, it can be done with a Philippine freelancer for around $300 a month.

Two popular Philippine websites for freelancers are:

http://BestJobs.ph
http://HireFilipino.com

One consideration that might temper your decision to hire fulltime freelancers is that you will have to manage them on a daily basis, just like an employee in any business.

When you outsourced the work you needed, you did it to gain free time to spend doing things that increase your bank account. Managing fulltime freelancers could take up a lot of your free time, which is what you were trying to avoid in the first place.

So, what do you do now? There are services online that manage your freelancers for you. You pay the company a monthly fee and they provide a qualified freelancer and then manage the freelancer for you, including sorting out the international legalities for you.

As with any service you hire, it can be an expensive option. The tradeoff is that the company manages your freelancer for you, relieving you of any responsibility other than paying the company's monthly fee.

And of course you have to manage the management company!

These two webmaster staffing websites manage fulltime freelancers for clients:

www.AgentsofValue.com
www.VirtualEmployee.com

Internet Marketing forums are great places to find freelancers looking for work. Many freelancers are members of marketing forums because that's where their target market is.

The Warrior Forum is one of the leading and maybe the most popular Internet marketing forum in existence today. They have a section for freelancers to advertise their services to a hungry public. If you start your own thread asking about freelancers, you could receive several replies in minutes.

Another way to find freelancers is to browse forums in the niche market you are in, other than Internet Marketing. Keep an eye on those members who post useful information on a regular basis and ask them if they would like to write some content for you.

Now that you know where to find reliable outsourcing, lets look at the process of finding a freelancer to work for you.

Do You Know How to Outsource?

Let's use Elance.com as an example of the entire process of outsourcing your work to freelancers on that site. Elance.com is very popular with Internet marketers.

When you are first starting out with freelancers, start small. If you need a series of articles written, hire two freelance writers and split the job between them. That way you can compare quality and speed of completion before you pick the more capable writer to work for you.

Opening an account on a freelance site, including Elance.com, is pretty easy and straight forward on most sites. After you open an account you will have to choose your payment method for your freelancers. PayPal is very popular worldwide and easy to use. Keep it easy.

After you confirm your account, you can post a job. Click the "Post Job" tab on the front page after you login.

Your next page will be where you enter some details about your project.

It is not necessary to exaggerate your title on this form. Just make it clear and pertinent to the job you are posting. Your title on this form is to provide a clear picture of what you want.

If you want 10 500-word articles, for example, about babies, a perfect title would be "10X500 word articles about babies needed." The freelancers looking for work would know exactly what you want and would click through if they wanted more details. You would be getting freelancers with a targeted interest in your subject.

Choose your category from the list of available categories. In this case, your choice would be "writing." Make sure you post in the most relevant category so interested writers can find your post.

After choosing the category, write your job description. This might be the most important part of posting your job. Make your description short and professional. Do not use jargon. Just plain words answering a few questions:

  o What exactly does the job include?

- Will help be available from you?

- What guidelines they will have to follow?

- When you want the finished copy?

- What's the Checkpoint date, if any?

- What qualities are you looking for in the freelancer you are going to hire?

- Is this a one-time job or is future work a possibility for the winning bidder?

Let's take a closer look at each question.

This one is the most important part of your job post. Be as clear as possible. You should start it off with something like... "I require someone to complete..." then tell them exactly what you need.

Do not leave out any details. If you want article writing... tell them how many you need, what the word count should be, keyword density, what style of writing should be used, what the articles are going to be used for.

If programming is your reason for needing a freelancer, tell them exactly what programming language should be used, what operating systems the program should work on, if the program is going to be web based etc.

If you don't know how to describe your job offer, then perform simple searches for a similar job posting so you can see how other employers are describing their offers. Copy Success!

Your freelancers will need to know what you're going to provide them with. That could be a list of keywords, possible titles and any research you have.

You will need to provide guidelines to keep your freelancer on track. If your needs and expectations are not spelled out in a clear manner your freelancer will not know what you want. Be crystal clear and specific. You can outline font size and color, for instance.

Make sure you have an achievable deadline. It will help the freelancer by letting them know when you want it. It will help you because you will be working with a deadline date that will allow you to plan your business actions.

Checkpoint dates are handy for keeping your project moving along in an organized manner. If your job is a large one, you might want to include checkpoint dates to keep close track of the progress.

When selecting a freelance writer, chose one who is knowledgeable with the subject. If your subject is gardening, hire a freelancer who knows gardening. If you want a programmer to produce your software, check their qualifications closely.

Future work is a major incentive for many freelancers and, if you mention the possibility of future work in your posting, that might get you lower bids because the freelancers will want to attract you for the future business.

If you have documents to use with your job, attach them to your offer. A spreadsheet with article titles and the keywords you want used would be helpful.

When you are finished with the job description, you will need to fill out the skill option. Using the article writing example, you may require someone with specific knowledge on your niche. Click the boxes beside the skills you need.

Your next option is selecting the job type. Here is where you indicate whether or not you are offering a freelancer a position in your company or just one job.

You have two decisions left to make, "Project" and "Position." The position option is used to offer a freelancer a fulltime position in your company and is rarely used. You don't need to use it to hire a freelancer fulltime. Just wait until your project is over and do it directly with the freelancer.

After you select the project option, your next selection is the payment option. Your choices are fixed fee or hourly. Select fixed fee. If a freelancer is working on an hourly fee, there is no incentive to work quickly. On the other hand, a freelancer working on a fixed fee will be inspired to get your project finished so he can move on to the next job.

Selecting fixed fee for a payment option requires that you set a budget for the project. If you don't know what to post for a budget, use a range like $50 -$500. If your project is larger or smaller than that budget allows, adjust the figures to suit your project.

Next, when asked to select where the freelancer will work, leave the selection on default. This entire process is online based and where a freelancer will work is not an option.

Elance uses the escrow system for payment. That means that when you have selected a winning bidder for your project, you will be required to pay the money to Elance. When the project is completed to your satisfaction, Elance will expect both of your to choose the "completed" option. Once that is finished, the freelancer will be paid.

The escrow system is good for both parties. The freelancer knows they are going to get paid when the project is finished and approved. You only approve the payment when the project is completed.

If you decide not to use the escrow system, you probably won't get many quality bids on your job.

Your final selection will be the advanced options.

USA citizens will need to tick the tax option, of course. You may want to tick the **"Seals Proposals"** option, which allows you to keep your bids private. Since freelancers cannot see what their competitors are bidding, you will get a fair bidding price. If you don't check the Seals Proposals option, the first bid will set the tone for the rest of the bids.

When you are finished, your job will be posted for all to see.

Choosing the winner...

It's a good idea to let your job run for at least 48 hours before selecting a winner.

Don't jump on the first decent bid you get. Others might make decent bids, too.

Once 48 hours is up, you'll see the bids that freelancers have made...

When selecting a winner, consider three factors, the quality of the feedback your bidder have received, their portfolio and experience and the bids made.

Experience is a critical consideration when choosing between bidders. Look closely at bidders with at least 10 positive feedback comments, which lets you know that the bidder has completed at least 10 jobs.

Percentage scores left for freelancers by employers are not a good way to judge the experience and ability of freelancers. Most of them will have percentages over 90%. One might have a lower percentage because of some confusion with what the employer wanted.

On the bidding page, you can click on the freelancer's name in blue to get to their profile page. Here you will see all their qualifications and experience, like an online resume.

Your next stop should be their portfolio, where you can see examples of their work.

Your last consideration is the bid price they entered. After checking out their feedback, profile and portfolio, you should have a pretty good idea about who is best suited for your project. If you like the quality you saw, check to see if their bid price is reasonable. If you think the freelancer is worth what they want to charge, you have a winner.

It is not a good idea to just select the lowest bidder unless, in your opinion, they can produce the quality work you want. If your first choice has priced his work out of your budget, pick one with good feedback, a quality profile and portfolio and an average bid.

In a nutshell, pick your freelancer offering the best value.

After your selection of the winner, you will have to set up checkpoints if you are using the escrow system. If you are ordering articles, you set how many you want on a daily basis. The freelancer gets paid daily when your checkpoint requirements are met, for example.

Keep all your communication with the freelancer within Elance. When you communication is outside of Elance, there will be no proof of what's happening and Elance will be unable to prove what happened if something goes wrong.

Elance handles problems between you and your freelancer, if they should crop up, if you have kept your communication inside Elance.

If a freelancer didn't finish the job or make the corrections you asked for, email Elance and they will take care of it. Only release the funds in escrow when you are satisfied with the work. If the freelancer refuses to make the corrections you pointed out, Elance will refund your money.

When you are satisfied and the freelancer has done the work to a high standard, leave feedback for him or her. Positive feedback is important to every freelancer and they would appreciate some left by you.

If you need future work and want a certain freelancer to do it, you can ask to deal with them through email, but then the entire risk is on you. You can make another job offer on

Elance and make it by invitation only, which lets you choose who can bid on your new job.

By now you should be secure with the processes required by Elance to post jobs on their site. You probably have a good idea about what to outsource, where to outsource and how to outsource.

Let's move on to setting up automatic income streams with outsourcing.

How To Automate Income Streams With Freelancers

This is where you learn to blend your needs for outsourcing with methods that will save you time. When you first start outsourcing, you might be tempted to do one thing at a time, like sending one article at a time to your freelancer or using their talents to bookmark only one of your sites at a time.

This ties you to daily contact with the freelancer that includes getting in contact, telling him what to write, how many words you require and where to submit it. Since outsourcing is supposed to free you from tedious daily tasks, you are defeating the entire process of outsourcing in the first place. You are creating your own nightmare.

Instead of doing the daily contact and parceling out the work one piece at a time, email your freelancer every Monday and give him a week's worth of work. That way, you are doing the work once for the week instead of every day. You can request daily work to be emailed to you.

With this plan, you can check the work your freelancer is completing for you as it is done and can request a re-purpose if needed. Sometimes you will want an article, for example, rewritten for a different purpose than originally agreed to.

If you hire your freelancer to post your articles to directories or to submit content to blogs, you have just used your freelancer to set-up automated streams of income. The freelancer is doing all the work and you are only sending the work to be done to him once a week. And paying him, of course.

Rinse and repeat the process for all your tedious work tasks. Soon you will have several automated streams of income flowing into your account.

All you have to do is keep your freelancer supplied with the work you need.

One word of caution...keep the intimate details of your business private. You don't want anyone to know too much about your business, particularly someone who could replicate your processes and become competition for you. Consider splitting your work up between two or several freelancers.

Final Thoughts

You should have a really good idea by now about exactly what to do when you need outsourcing. Make a list of the tasks you enjoy, tasks that take up too much of your time and the tasks you just hate. From those lists, you can decide what you need to outsource.

When you first experiment with outsourcing, you are bound to run into problems that are out of your control. Bad experiences with freelancers are part of marketing and you would be well-advised to learn from them and move on to something productive. Your success depends on it.

Have fun and learn to make your load lighter by using freelancers. Your business will love it.

Once you're outsourced you won't go back!

www.ingramcontent.com/pod-product-compliance
Lightning Source LLC
Chambersburg PA
CBHW071239220526
45468CB00002B/931